2016 Calendar – Japan Outdoor Photos – Japanese Version

(Japan's National Holidays Shown)
(Full Moon Dates = ☺)

Copyright © 2015 Daniel H. Wieczorek & Kazuya Numazawa

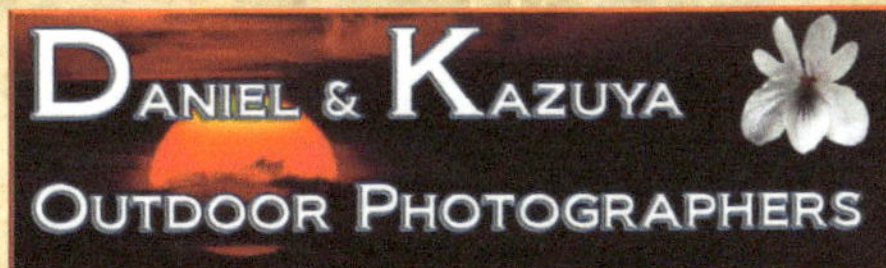

ISBN-10: 0996362649
ISBN-13: 978-0-9963626-4-1

PHOTOS INCLUDED IN THIS CALENDAR

January: An Ice Covered Hyakuhiro Waterfall. Western Tokyo, Japan.
February: A Beautiful Plum Tree at Kyodo-No- Mori Park. Fuchu City, Tokyo, Japan.
March: The Hakuba Mountains, from Tsugaike Kogen. Nagano Prefecture, Japan.
April: A Beautiful Cherry Tree in a Yard in the Foothills. Western Tokyo, Japan.
May: A Heavily Manipulated Photo of Mt. Fuji. Western Tokyo, Japan.
June: An Extremely Rare *Paeonia obovata* Found in a Secret Location. Eastern Japan.
July: Mt. Fuji, Taken from Kawaguchi Lake Station. Yamanashi Prefecture, Japan.
August: Mt. Hiuchigatake & Oze Marsh, Oze National Park. Fukushima Prefecture, Japan.
September: Mt. Chokai & Interesting Cloud Phenomenon. Yamagata/Akita Prefectures, Japan.
October: Mt. Fuji from the Okuniwa Area. Yamanashi Prefecture, Japan.
November: A Beautiful Red Maple at Jindai Botanical Garden. Tokyo, Japan.
December: "Diamond Fuji" – The Day the Sun Sets Behind Mt. Fuji – Taken at Summit of Mt. Takao. Tokyo, Japan.

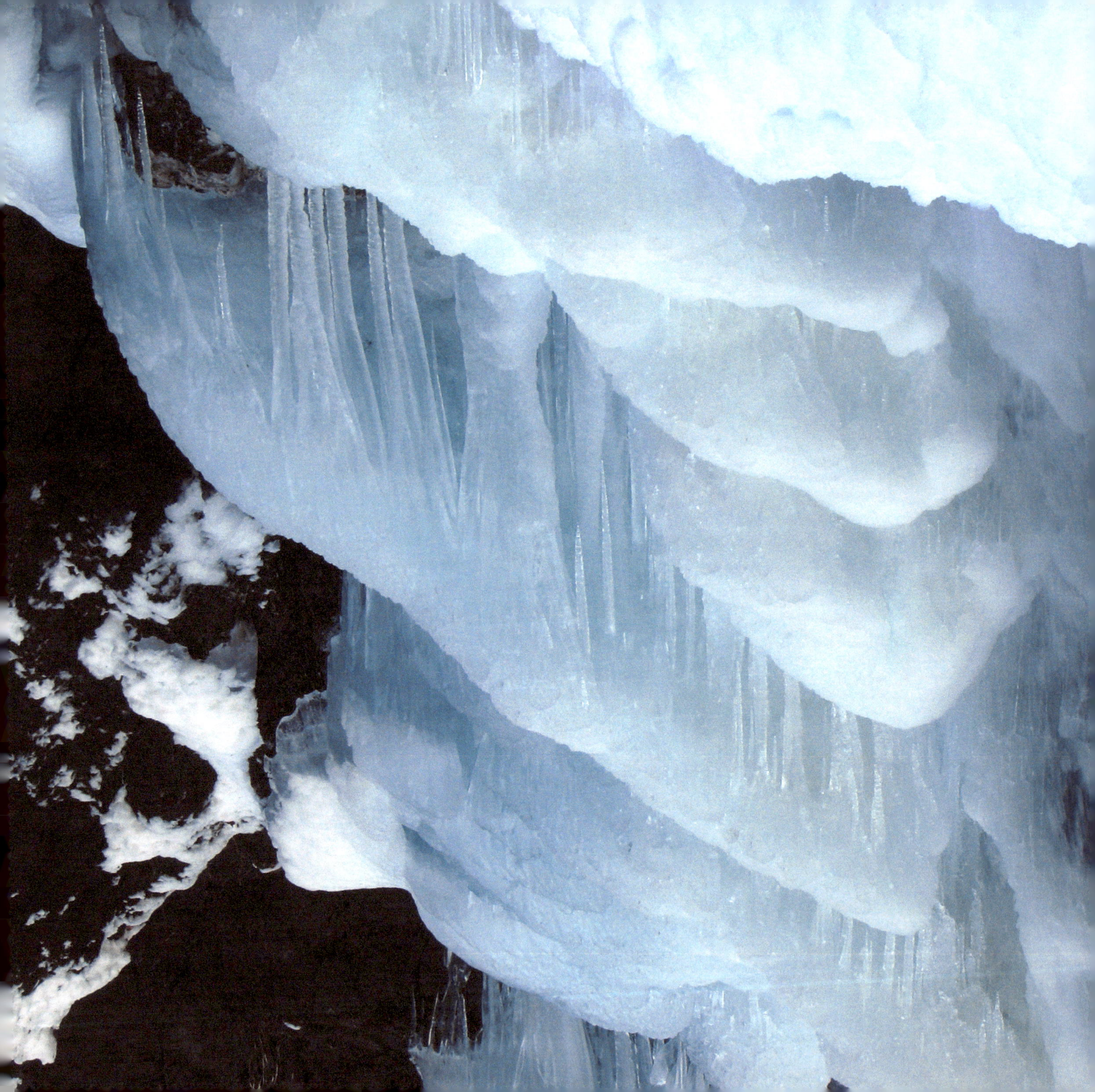

January | 2016

Sun	Mon	Tue	Wed	Thu	Fri	Sat
27	28	29	30	31	1 New Year's Day	2
3	4	5	6	7	8	9
10	11 Coming of Age Day	12	13	14	15	16
17	18	19	20	21	22	23
	25	26	27	28	29	30
31	1	2	3	4	5	6

An Ice Covered Hyakuhiro Waterfall. Western Tokyo, Japan.

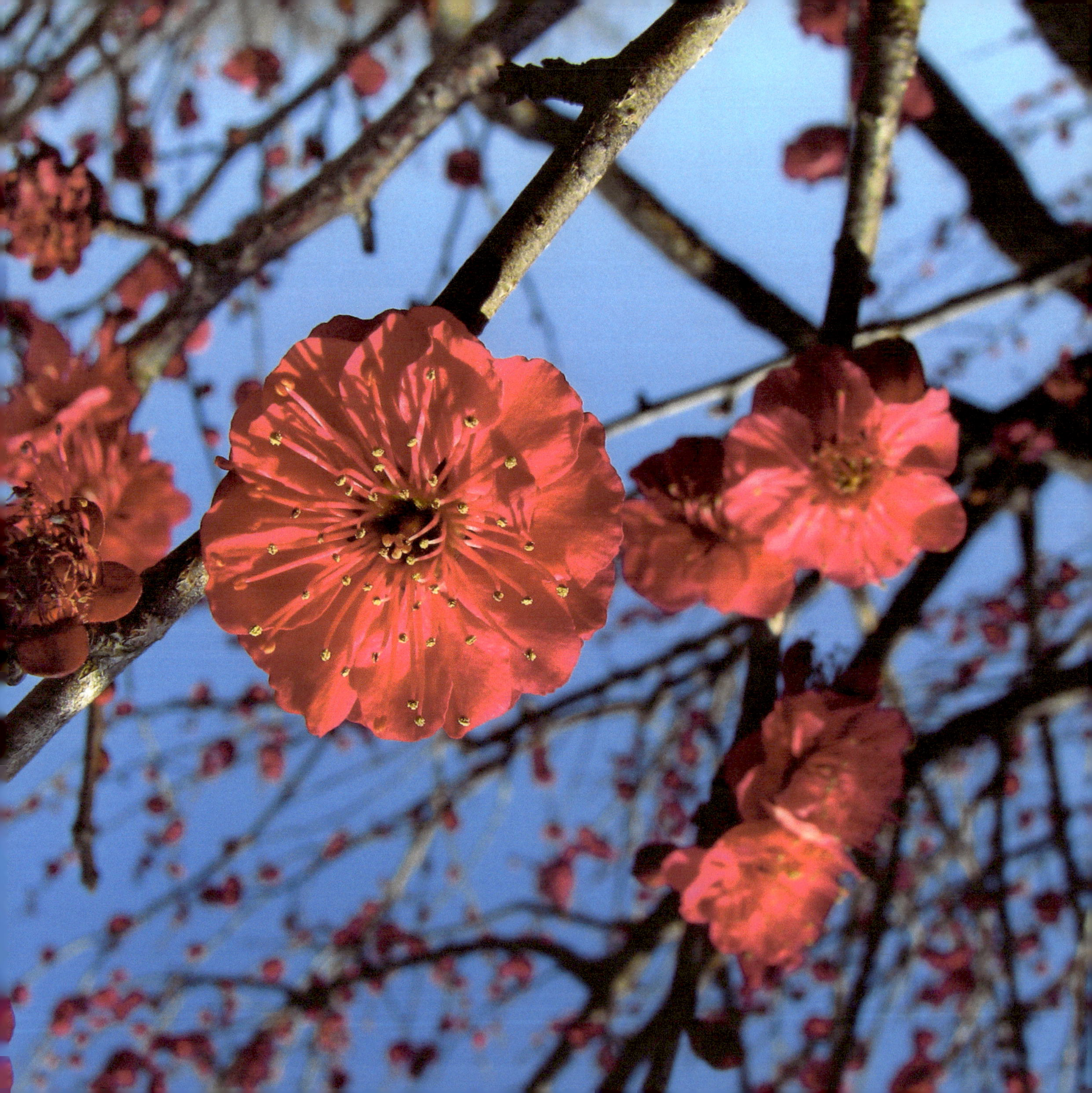

February 2016

Sun	Mon	Tue	Wed	Thu	Fri	Sat
31	1	2	3	4	5	6
7	8	9	10	11 National Foundation Day	12	13
14	15	16	17	18	19	20
21	22	☺	24	25	26	27
28	29	1	2	3	4	5

A Beautiful Plum Tree at Kyodo-No- Mori Park. Fuchu City, Tokyo, Japan.

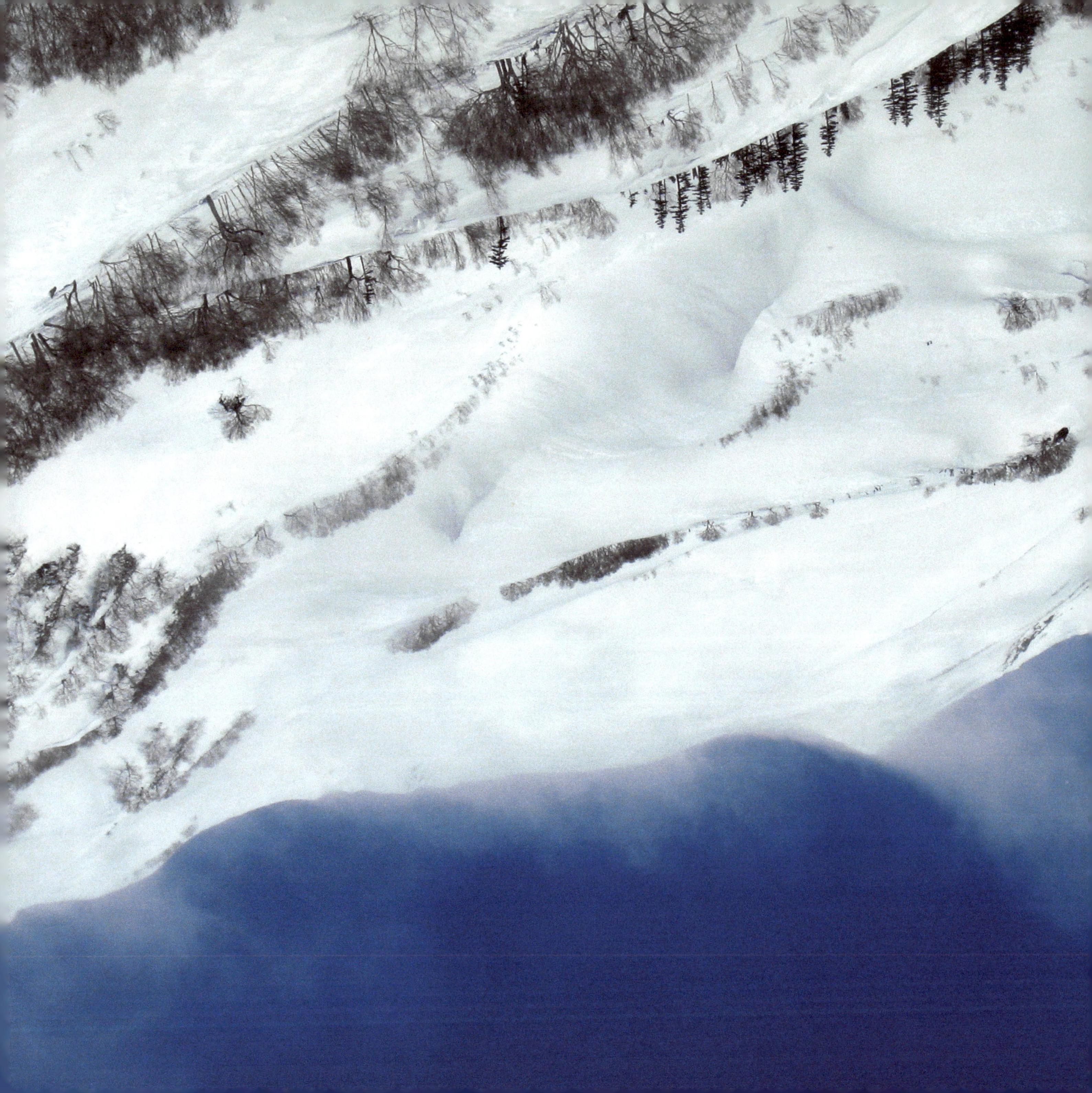

<table>
<tr><td colspan="7">March   2016</td></tr>
<tr><td>Sun</td><td>Mon</td><td>Tue</td><td>Wed</td><td>Thu</td><td>Fri</td><td>Sat</td></tr>
<tr><td>28</td><td>29</td><td>1</td><td>2</td><td>3</td><td>4</td><td>5</td></tr>
<tr><td>6</td><td>7</td><td>8</td><td>9</td><td>10</td><td>11</td><td>12</td></tr>
<tr><td>13</td><td>14</td><td>15</td><td>16</td><td>17</td><td>18</td><td>19</td></tr>
<tr><td>20
13:30 Japan Time
Vernal Equinox</td><td>21
Vernal Equinox
(observed)</td><td>22</td><td>🌝</td><td>24</td><td>25</td><td>26</td></tr>
<tr><td>27</td><td>28</td><td>29</td><td>30</td><td>31</td><td>1</td><td>2</td></tr>
</table>

The Hakuba Mountains, from Tsugaike Kogen. Nagano Prefecture, Japan.

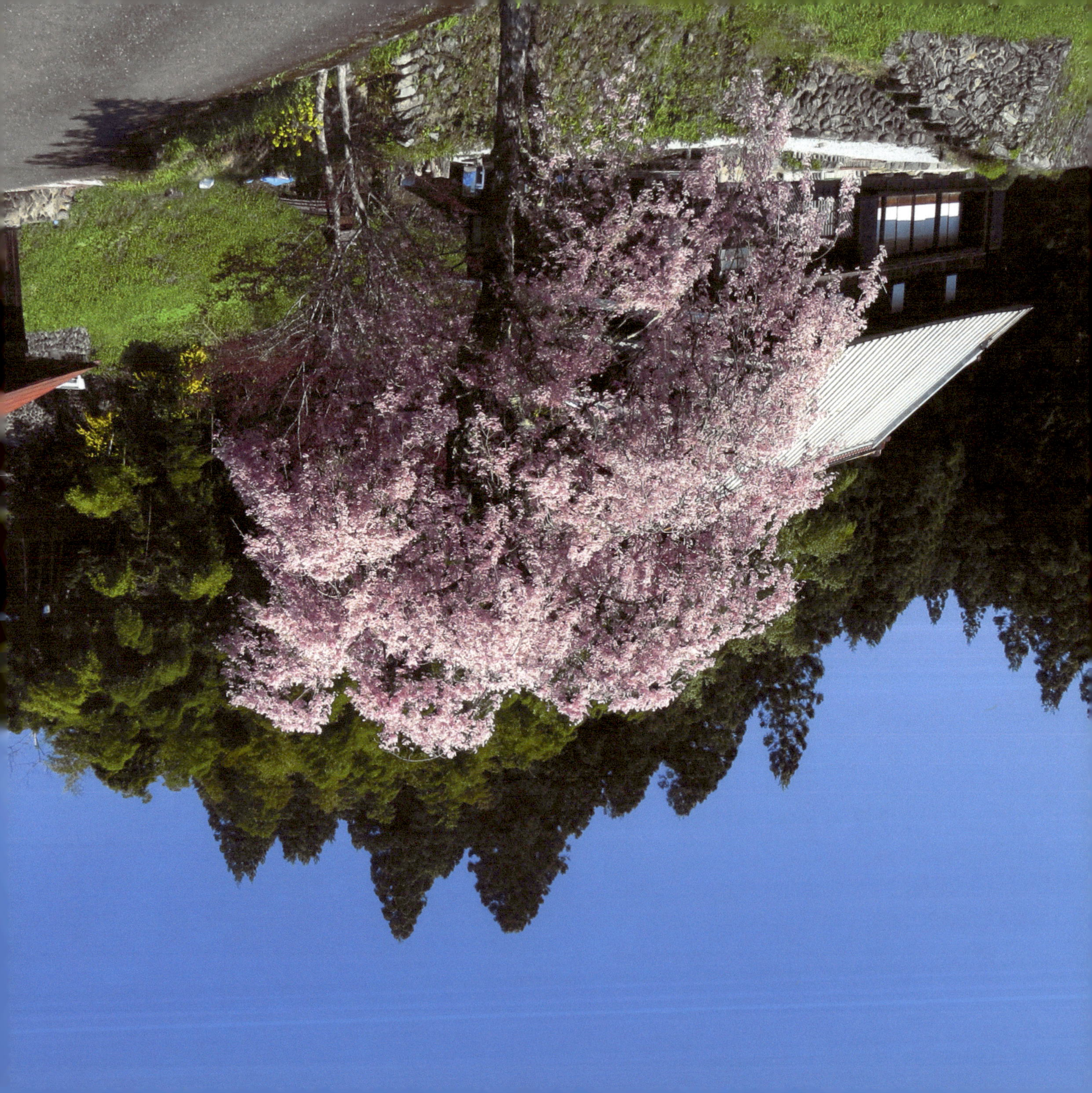

April 2016

Sun	Mon	Tue	Wed	Thu	Fri	Sat
27	28	29	30	31	1	2
3	4	5	6	7	8	9
10	11	12	13	14	15	16
17	18	19	20	21	☺	23
24	25	26	27	28	29 Shōwa Day	30

A Beautiful Cherry Tree in a Yard in the Foothills. Western Tokyo, Japan.

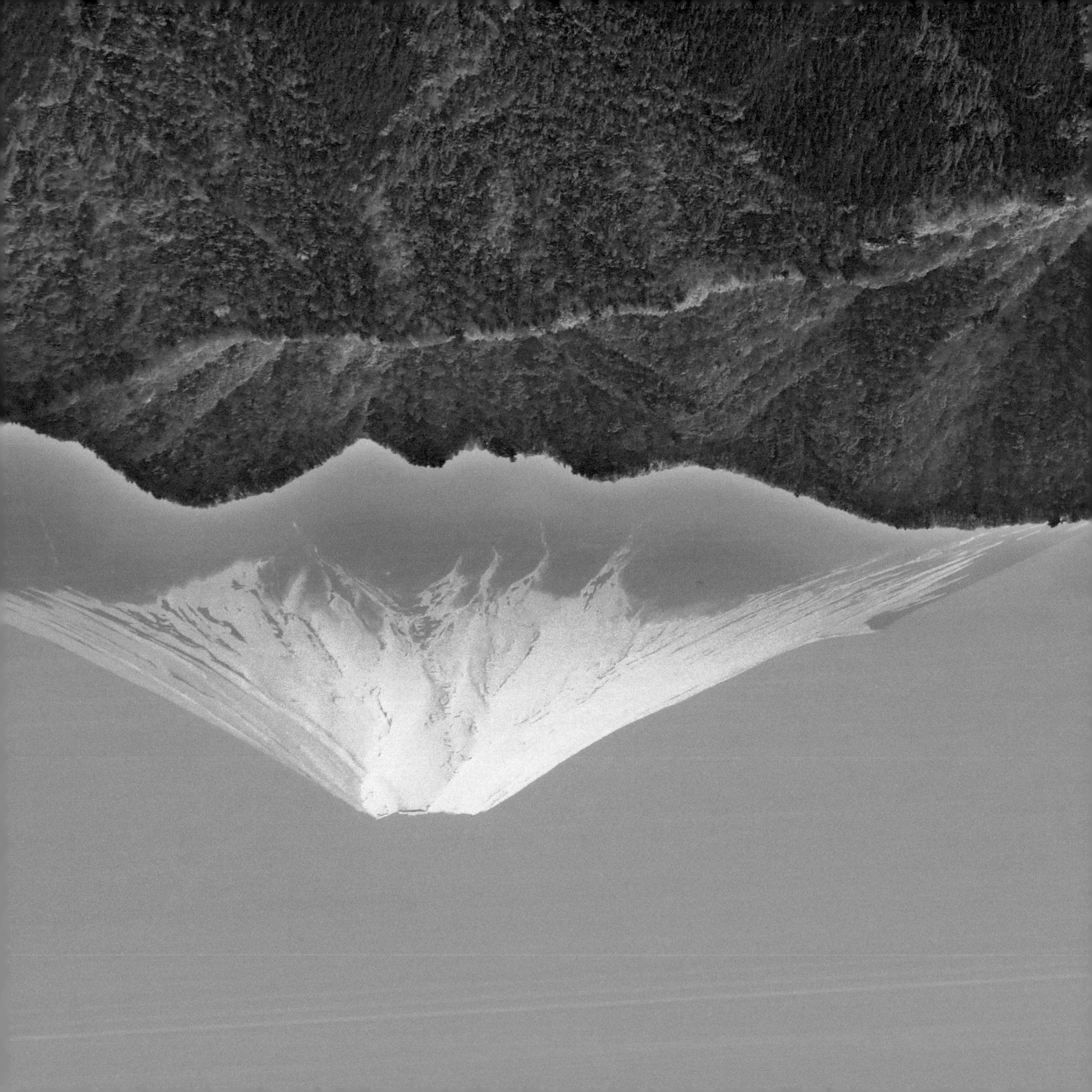

<table>
<tr><td colspan="2" align="center">May</td><td colspan="5" align="right">2016</td></tr>
<tr><th>Sun</th><th>Mon</th><th>Tue</th><th>Wed</th><th>Thu</th><th>Fri</th><th>Sat</th></tr>
<tr><td>1</td><td>2</td><td>3
Constitution Memorial Day</td><td>4
Greenery Day</td><td>5
Children's Day</td><td>6</td><td>7</td></tr>
<tr><td>8</td><td>9</td><td>10</td><td>11</td><td>12</td><td>13</td><td>14</td></tr>
<tr><td>15</td><td>16</td><td>17</td><td>18</td><td>19</td><td>20</td><td>21</td></tr>
<tr><td></td><td>23</td><td>24</td><td>25</td><td>26</td><td>27</td><td>28</td></tr>
<tr><td>29</td><td>30</td><td>31</td><td>1</td><td>2</td><td>3</td><td>4</td></tr>
</table>

A Heavily Manipulated Photo of Mt. Fuji. Western Tokyo, Japan.

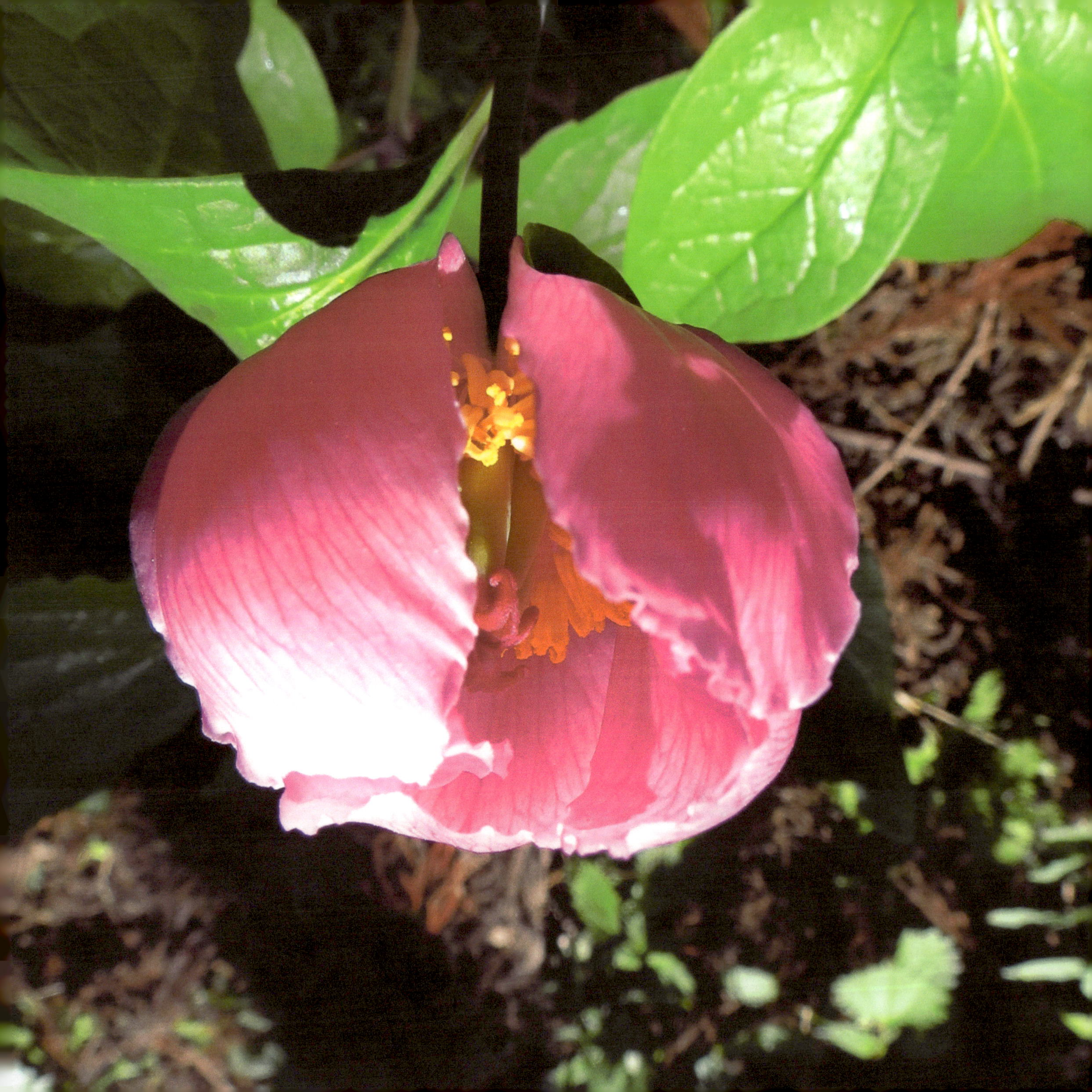

<table>
<tr><td colspan="2">**June**</td><td colspan="5" align="right">**2016**</td></tr>
<tr><td>**Sun**</td><td>**Mon**</td><td>**Tue**</td><td>**Wed**</td><td>**Thu**</td><td>**Fri**</td><td>**Sat**</td></tr>
<tr><td>29</td><td>30</td><td>31</td><td>1</td><td>2</td><td>3</td><td>4</td></tr>
<tr><td>5</td><td>6</td><td>7</td><td>8</td><td>9</td><td>10</td><td>11</td></tr>
<tr><td>12</td><td>13</td><td>14</td><td>15</td><td>16</td><td>17</td><td>18</td></tr>
<tr><td>19</td><td>☻</td><td>21
**07:34 Japan Time
Summer Solstice**</td><td>22</td><td>23</td><td>24</td><td>25</td></tr>
<tr><td>26</td><td>27</td><td>28</td><td>29</td><td>30</td><td>1</td><td>2</td></tr>
</table>

An Extremely Rare *Paeonia obovata* Found in a Secret Location. Eastern Japan.

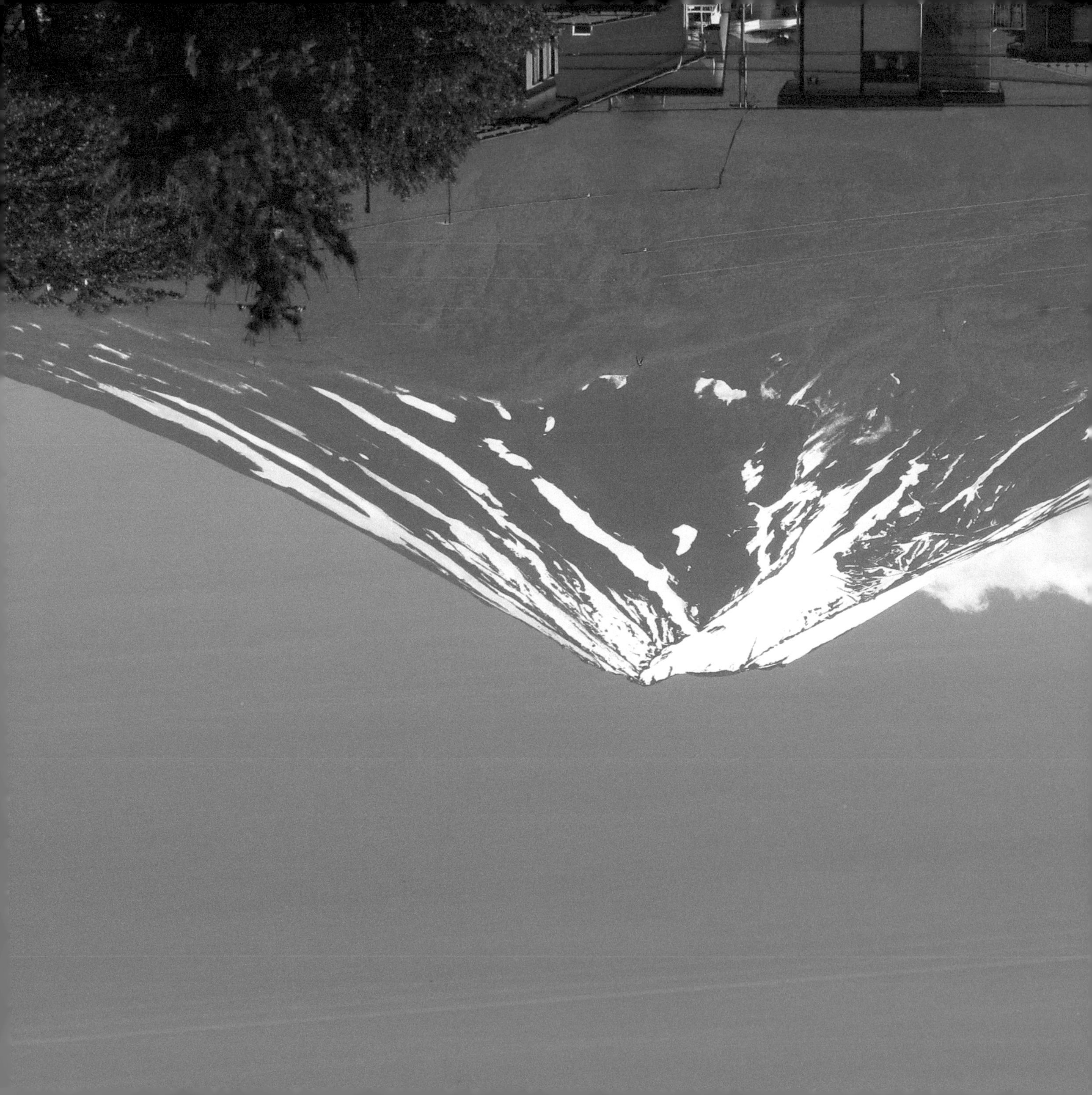

July 2016

Sun	Mon	Tue	Wed	Thu	Fri	Sat
26	27	28	29	30	1	2
3	4	5	6	7	8	9
10	11	12	13	14	15	16
17	18 Sea Day	19	🌝	21	22	23
24	25	26	27	28	29	30
31	1	2	3	4	5	6

Mt. Fuji, Taken from Kawaguchi Lake Station. Yamanashi Prefecture, Japan.

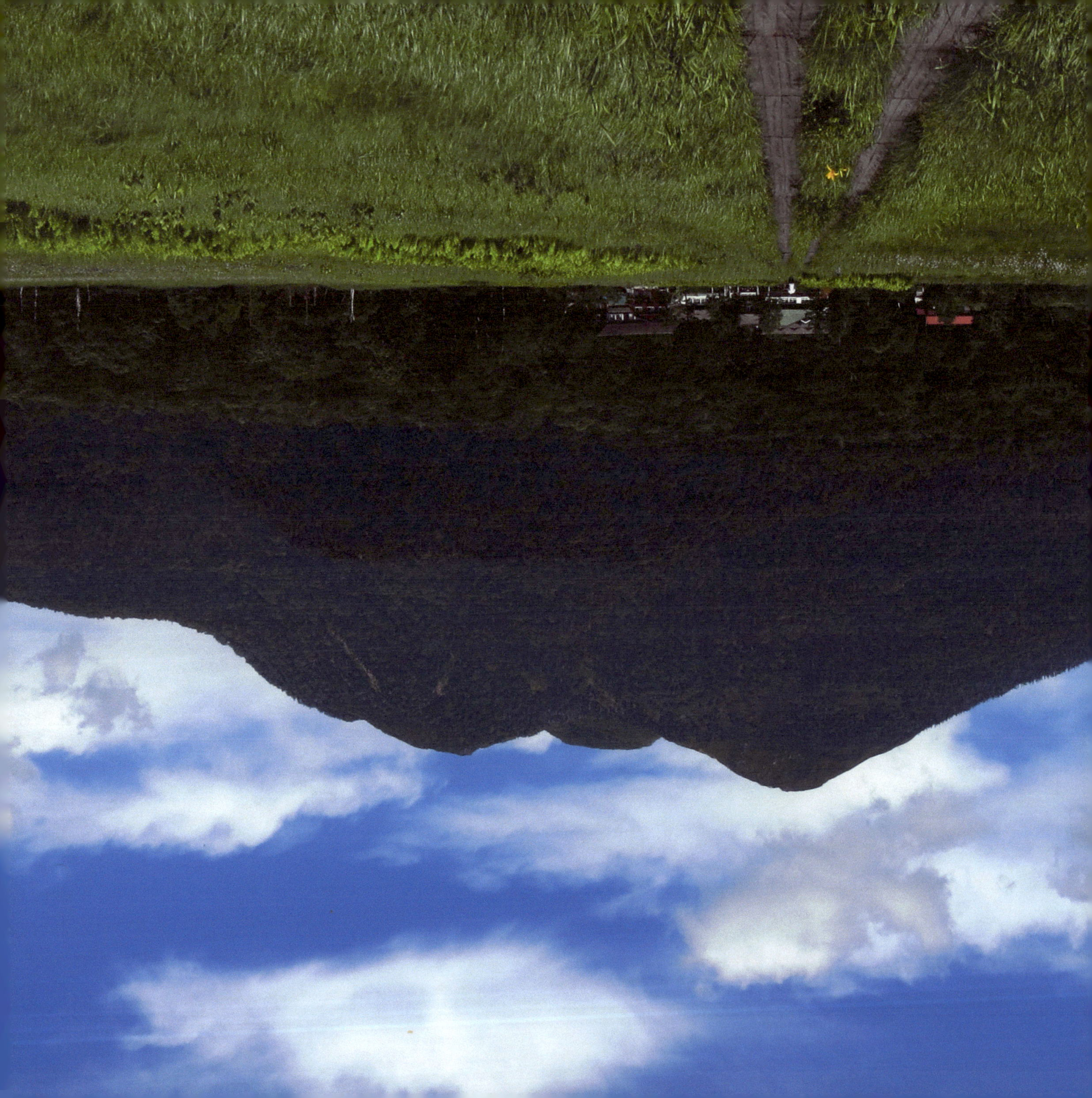

August 2016

Sun	Mon	Tue	Wed	Thu	Fri	Sat
31	1	2	3	4	5	6
7	8	9	10	11 **Mountain Day**	12	13
14	15	16	17	18	19	20
21	22	23	24	25	26	27
28	29	30	31	1	2	3

Mt. Hiuchigatake & Oze Marsh, Oze National Park. Fukushima Prefecture, Japan.

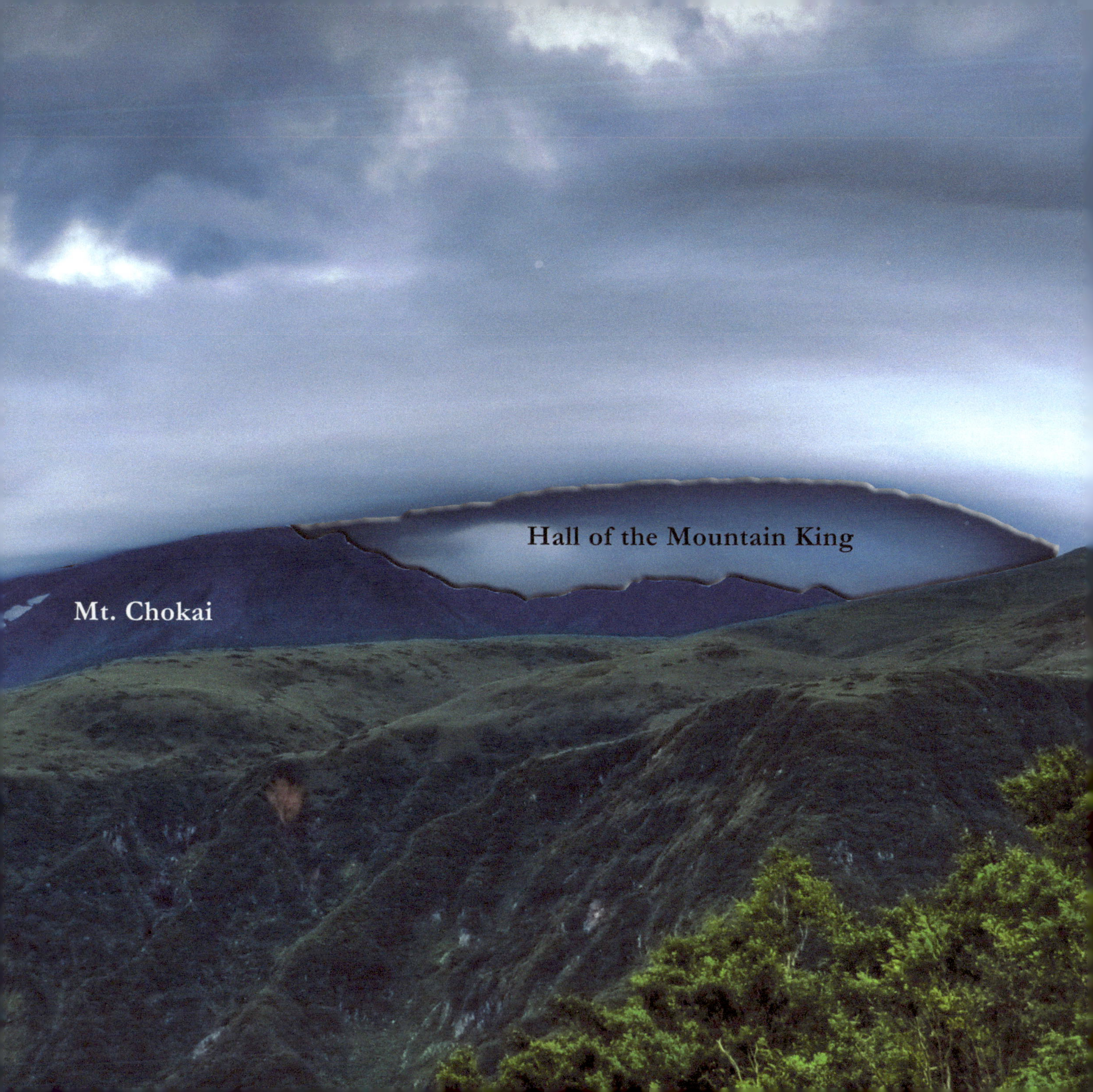

Hall of the Mountain King
Mt. Chokai

September   2016

Sun	Mon	Tue	Wed	Thu	Fri	Sat
28	29	30	31	1	2	3
4	5	6	7	8	9	10
11	12	13	14	15	16	
18	19 **Respect for the Aged Day**	20	21	22 **23:21 Japan Time Autumnal Equinox**	23	24
25	26	27	28	29	30	1

Mt. Chokai & Interesting Cloud Phenomenon. Yamagata/Akita Prefectures, Japan.

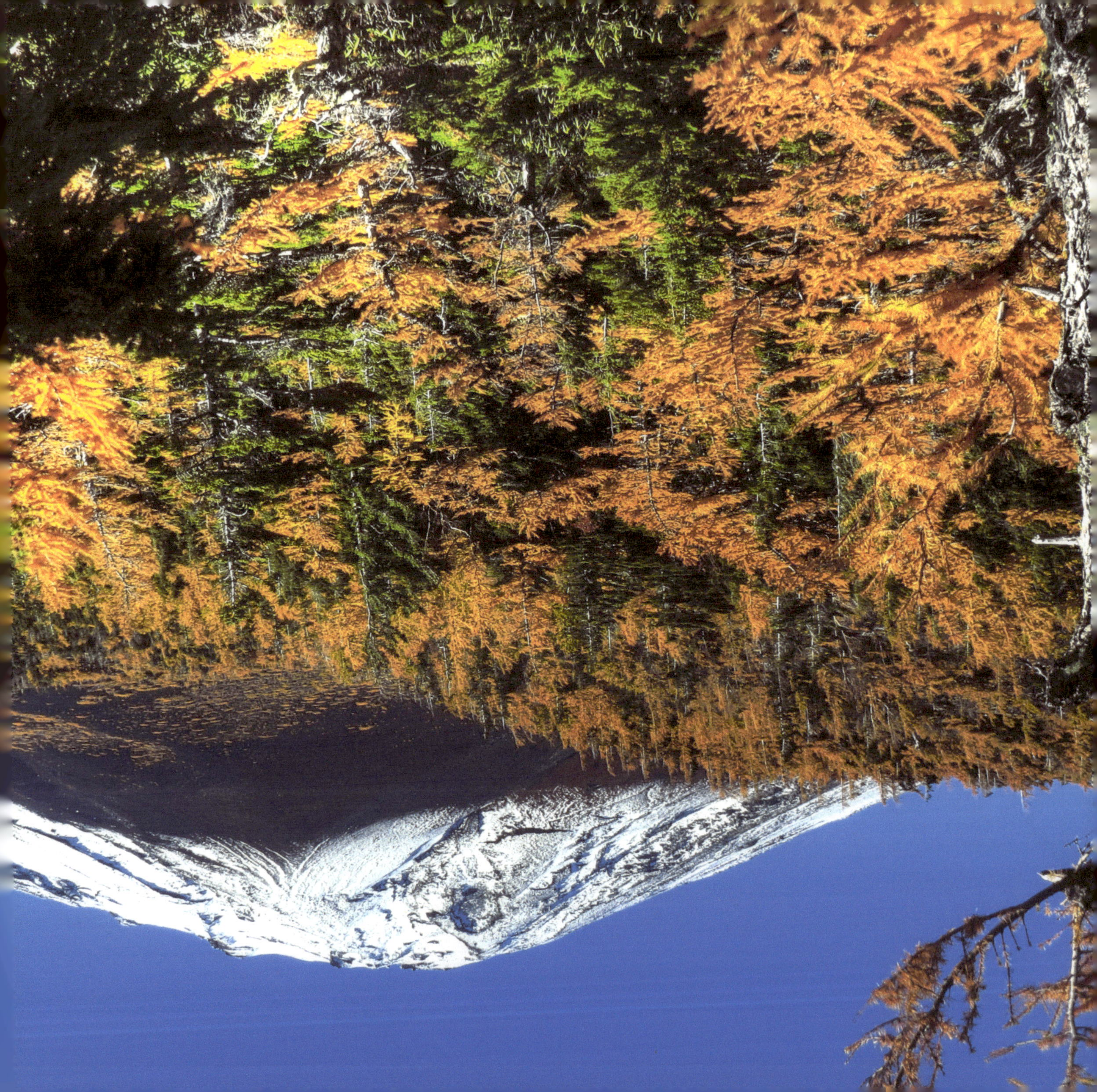

October 2016

Sun	Mon	Tue	Wed	Thu	Fri	Sat
25	26	27	28	29	30	1
2	3	4	5	6	7	8
9	10 Sports Day	11	12	13	14	15
	17	18	19	20	21	22
23	24	25	26	27	28	29
30	31	1	2	3	4	5

Mt. Fuji from the Okuniwa Area. Yamanashi Prefecture, Japan.

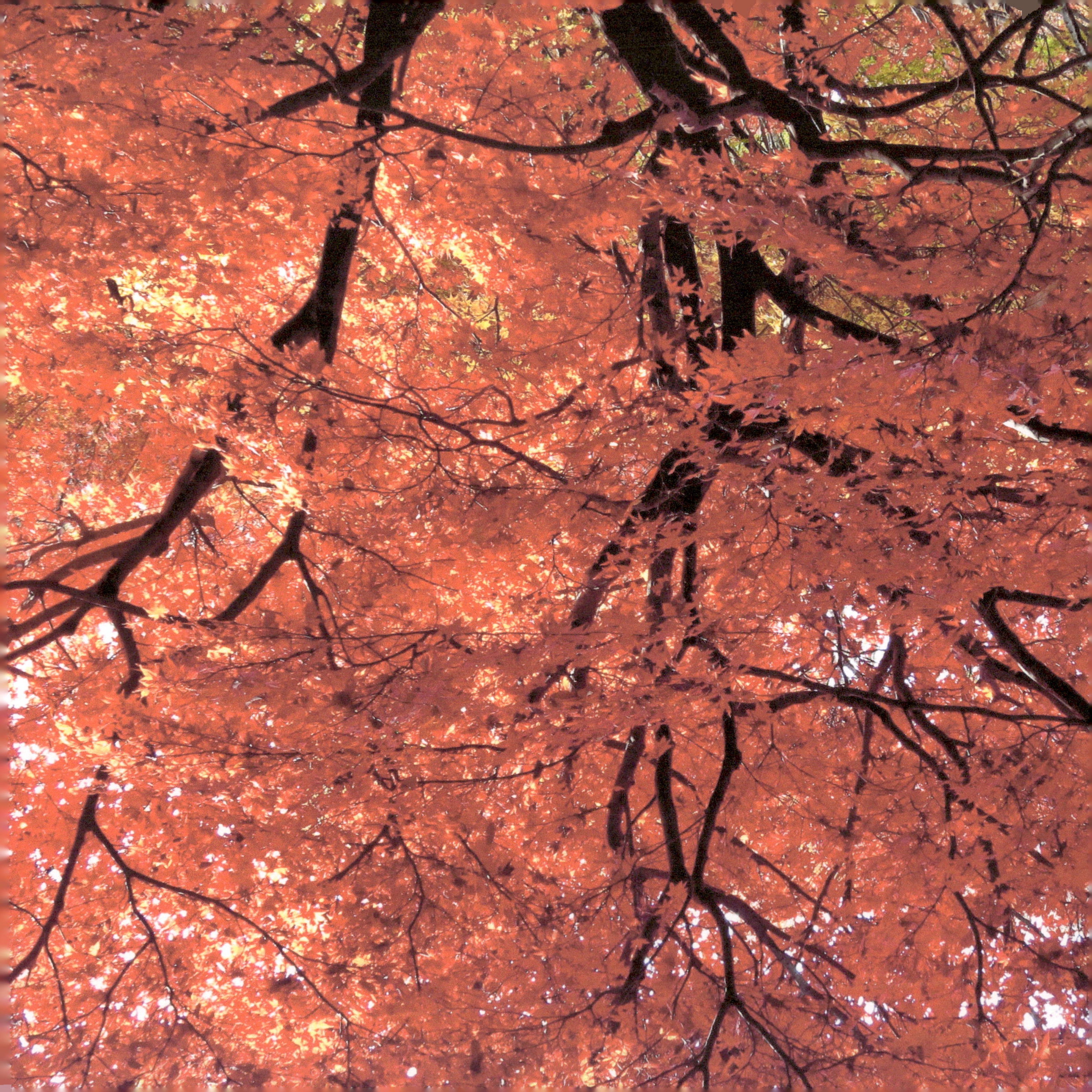

November 2016

Sun	Mon	Tue	Wed	Thu	Fri	Sat
30	31	1	2	3 Culture Day	4	5
6	7	8	9	10	11	12
13	☺	15	16	17	18	19
20	21	22	23 Labor Thanksgiving Day	24	25	26
27	28	29	30	1	2	3

A Beautiful Red Maple at Jindai Botanical Garden. Tokyo, Japan.

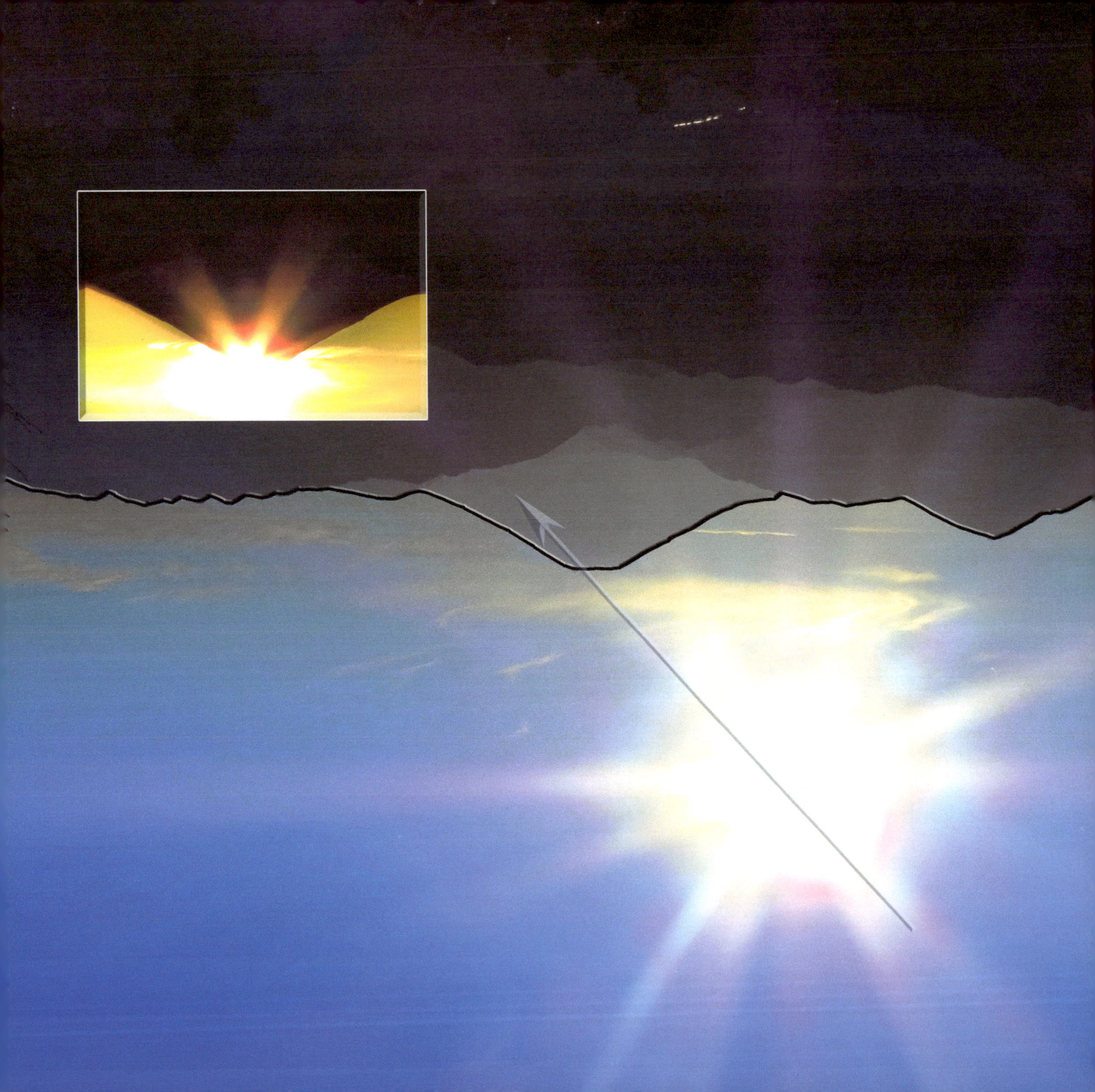

December 2016

Sun	Mon	Tue	Wed	Thu	Fri	Sat
27	28	29	30	1	2	3
4	5	6	7	8	9	10
11	12	13	☺	15	16	17
18	19	20	21 **19:44 Japan Time Winter Solstice**	22	23 **Emperor's Birthday**	24
25	26	27	28	29	30	31

"Diamond Fuji" – The Day the Sun Sets Behind Mt. Fuji – Taken at Summit of Mt. Takao. Tokyo, Japan.
Gray arrow shows path of sun. Inset photo taken 22 minutes after main photo.

2016 Phases of the Moon

Japan Time

New Moon				First Quarter				Full Moon				Last Quarter			
	d	h	m		d	h	m		d	h	m		d	h	m
--	--	--	--	--	--	--	--	--	--	--	--	JAN	02	14	30
JAN	10	10	30	JAN	17	07	26	JAN	24	10	46	FEB	01	12	28
FEB	08	23	39	FEB	15	16	46	FEB	23	03	20	MAR	02	08	11
MAR	09	10	54	MAR	16	02	03	MAR	23	21	01	APR	01	00	17
APR	07	20	24	APR	14	12	59	APR	22	14	24	APR	30	12	29
MAY	07	04	29	MAY	14	02	02	MAY	22	06	14	MAY	29	21	12
JUN	05	12	00	JUN	12	17	10	JUN	20	21	02	JUN	28	03	19
JUL	04	20	01	JUL	12	09	52	JUL	20	07	56	JUL	27	08	00
AUG	03	05	44	AUG	11	03	21	AUG	18	18	26	AUG	25	12	41
SEP	01	18	03	SEP	09	19	49	SEP	17	04	05	SEP	23	18	56
OCT	01	09	11	OCT	09	13	33	OCT	16	13	23	OCT	23	04	14
OCT	31	02	38	NOV	03	04	51	NOV	14	22	52	NOV	21	17	33
NOV	29	21	18	DEC	07	18	03	DEC	14	09	05	DEC	21	10	56
DEC	29	15	53	--	--	--	--	--	--	--	--	--	--	--	--

Earth's Seasons – 2016

JapanTime

		d	h			d	h	m		d	h	m
Perihelion	Jan	03	08	Equinoxes	Mar	20	13	30	Sept	22	23	21
Aphelion	July	05	01	Solstices	June	21	07	34	Dec	21	19	44

If you enjoyed the photographs shown in this calendar then please be sure to check out our website. It can be found at http://danwiz.com. As long as he is alive he hopes to be able to maintain it.

Kazuya's blog can be found at: http://studiesofplantsandwildlife.blogspot.com or alternately, http://www2.blogger.com/profile/02622643778290337101.